Endorsement

Prayer That Sparks National Revival is a prophetic declaration of how we move from the miracle of the 2016 election to allowing God's promises to continue. Wanda accurately portrays the spiritual reality we are living in while prescribing the intercessory solution for the future. Most prophetic voices and authors focus on the veracity of our decrees while Wanda's focus is appropriately personal resulting in real results. The quick read is a must.

—David Kubal
President and CEO
Intercessors for America

PRAYER
THAT SPARKS
NATIONAL
REVIVAL

AN ESSENTIAL GUIDE FOR
RECLAIMING AMERICA'S DESTINY

PRAYER
THAT SPARKS
NATIONAL
REVIVAL

WANDA ALGER

DESTINY IMAGE® PUBLISHERS, INC.
P.O. Box 310, Shippensburg, PA 17257-0310
"Promoting Inspired Lives."

This book and all other Destiny Image and Destiny Image Fiction books are available at Christian bookstores and distributors worldwide.

Cover design by Eileen Rockwell

For more information on foreign distributors, call 717-532-3040.

Reach us on the Internet: www.destinyimage.com.

ISBN 13 TP: 978-0-7684-5301-0

ISBN 13 eBook: 978-0-7684-5302-7

For Worldwide Distribution, Printed in the U.S.A.

1 2 3 4 5 6 7 8 / 23 22 21 20 19

Contents

THE CURRENT STATE
OF THE CHURCH AND CALL FOR
RIGHTEOUS RULERS

THE election of Donald J. Trump to the presidency in 2016 was an historic event, not only for our nation but for the body of Christ. Never before has there been such engagement in the electoral process on such a wide scale. Nor has there ever been as much heated debate and division among believers concerning a national election.

In addition to the multitudes of voices yelling from the sidelines on social media, many unsuspecting citizens fell prey to the liberal media's bait, selling a false narrative that dominated the news cycles even more than the actual facts. Many who found themselves lost in the sea of public opinion and media debate struggled to determine what was true and what was false.

Those who discerned the process from the unseen realm, however, saw something else. They saw a spiritual battle that was raging, far deadlier than the earthly one. The demonic forces at work behind the scenes were feeding a storm between the people of God and those who vehemently opposed Him. Those who had been praying from the watchtowers of their homes and communities for years saw the anti-Christ agenda at work systematically and methodically undermining the very roots of our Judeo-Christian foundation.

These watchmen and intercessors have increasingly become emboldened in their prayers and fearless in their determination to open people's eyes to the true battle at hand. Many prophetic voices have been warning the Church of the spiritual strongholds at work in the high places of our nation in hopes of awakening those who have lapsed to the sidelines. If there was ever any doubt of spiritual warfare and the underlying demonic agenda lurking beneath the surface of our government, the 2016 election brought things to the surface as never before.

THE NEED FOR 2020 VISION

Thankfully, the prayers of the saints prevailed in 2016 and the evil forces seeking to hijack our nation through the highest office in the land were thwarted. At least temporarily. Believers have come to realize that the Adversary does not give up easily nor without a fight. Even though the victory of Donald J. Trump to the presidency has brought some long-needed changes and a measure of God-fearing rule to our nation, it has also brought some challenging barriers.

On the positive side, the issue of faith in the public square has become a worthy cause. Conservative Christians are increasingly unashamed in voicing their conviction about godly leadership in government and the need for faith to influence the public square. Prayer has become a tangible force as believers across the body of Christ have started to engage in the political process. Seeing our core biblical values threatened as never before, many evangelicals are speaking loud and clear demanding leaders with character, integrity, and accountability.

Unfortunately, this very value has presented challenges for some believers with Donald Trump's leadership style. For those who were looking for a leader with a clean record and pastoral approach to the presidency, Trump has been the bull in the china store. Even after his election, many believers have been offended by his style, his methods, and his language. Regardless of the obvious economic advances of his administration or delivery of campaign promises, his leadership has been anything but predictable or "presidential." The polarizing effect he has had on many in the Church has continued to grow and widen, thus making the quest for unity even greater.

This division comes from fiercely debated values as Republican believers are being challenged, not only by radical non-believers but by Democrat-leaning Christians. The conservative biblical worldview is no longer the righteous standard among some in the Church. The call for social justice, gender equality, and helping the poor has become the presumed hallmark of Jesus' teachings instead of living a holy life. To challenge this stance is to appear religious, arrogant, and biased. Thus, our need for greater clarity of vision, understanding of purpose, and conviction of truth.

THE CALL FOR RIGHTEOUS RULERS

For those who have eyes to see, we as believers have the opportunity before us to take our place as leaders in this nation—right in the middle of enemy territory.

The Lord says to my Lord: "Sit at my right hand, until I make your enemies your footstool." The Lord sends forth from Zion your mighty scepter. Rule in the midst of your enemies! (Psalms 110:1-2 ESV)

The kind of prayer that sparks national revival starts with a righteous remnant, those who take a stand for holiness and purity before the Lord. It takes courageous men and women to stand for what is true and good and not allow threats or accusations to silence their voice, either in the secret place or in the public square.

There is no true transformation without holiness and there is no cultural shift apart from the fear of the Lord. Change must first take place in our own hearts and be reflected by prayers that are effective and powerful. Those prayers, however, must go beyond personal desire to corporate agreement. And this is where our greatest challenge lies. We need to find common ground in the midst of extremist views and rhetoric so we can rise with one voice and one message. This is the only way the Ekklesia will have any Kingdom authority in the governmental sphere.

As we consider the future before us, we need to have a clear vision as the Church and the task before us. Though tribulations increase around the globe, we have been given a commission. Rather than preparing to leave, we should be positioned to lead. Instead of predicting the end, we should be presenting our case. Rather than storing up provisions for fear of impending doom, we should be out in our communities releasing the clarity, purpose, and wisdom that our culture so desperately needs. Though Jesus clearly said to be ready for His return, His primary message was to preach the gospel, demonstrate the Kingdom, and bring order to the earth He gave us to steward (see Mark 16:15; Luke 4:43; Gen. 1:28).

Good government rises and falls on leadership. This is true in both the sacred and secular realms. The dysfunctional leadership now in some of the highest positions of our government is, unfortunately, a reflection of the Church's fractured leadership. This is not from lack of love for God or even love for others. It's due to immaturity of character and lack of accountability in leadership. The fatherless generation talked about for decades is now grown up and seeking positions of power and influence. Without a solid biblical worldview and a community of faith in place, we will continue to see wicked rulers rise and Kingdom expression censored.

If we are to find common ground to gain 2020 vision for our future, we must start in the place of prayer. We must surrender our personal preferences, our biased opinions, and our sacred cows. We must be willing to agree on that which is most vital in order for the Ekklesia to rise in the land and provide light in the darkness.

+ We must pray with pure hearts, clean hands, and the mind of Christ.

+ We must pray with the kind of oneness that bears fruit (see 1 Cor. 1:10).

+ We must fix our eyes not on what is seen, but on what is unseen (see 2 Cor. 4:18).

+ We must judge things from heaven's perspective and not our own.

+ We must acknowledge the demonic forces at work in the roots of our nation and grow in corporate authority to displace these wicked rulers in high places.

As more and more believers are sensing the desperation of the hour and the need for prayer, here are twelve principles of righteous intercession that can help unify our goals. As we come into agreement with God's Word and humble ourselves to His will and purpose, He can do that which we cannot—bind us together through the unity of the Spirit (see Eph. 4:1-6). By God's grace, may we reason together and hear from heaven in order

to align our hearts, renew our minds, and demonstrate the Kingdom through our actions.

12-DAY
PRAYER GUIDE FOR 2020
VISION

USE these 12 prayer points to help the Church focus our vision for clear 2020 vision in this next election cycle.

Prayerfully consider how each of these truths affects your own life and witness and then pray for the body of Christ to walk in similar freedom.

DAY 1:

Remove the Roadblocks

> *Build up, build up, prepare the road!*
> *Remove the obstacles out of the way*
> *of my people* (Isaiah 57:14).

1. Repent for past mistakes including apathy, denial, rebellion, and independence.

Come near to God and he will come near to you. Wash your hands, you sinners, and purify your hearts, you double-minded. Grieve, mourn and wail. Change your laughter to mourning and your joy to gloom. Humble yourselves before the Lord, and he will lift you up (James 4:8-10).

2. Ask the Lord for fresh insight into roadblocks and obstacles; acknowledge them and apply His mercy.

You have set our iniquities before you, our secret sins in the light of your presence (Psalms 90:8).

3. Look for where God is working and where He is blessing; surrender any personal agenda for Kingdom purposes.

Bear fruit in keeping with repentance (Matthew 3:8 ESV).

DAY 2:

Invite the Fear of the Lord

> *Who, then, are those who fear the Lord?*
> *He will instruct them in the ways they*
> *should choose. They will spend their days*
> *in prosperity, and their descendants will*
> *inherit the land. The Lord confides in*
> *those who fear him; he makes his covenant*
> *known to them* (Psalms 25:12-14).

1. **P**ray for our nation to walk in the fear of the Lord and the knowledge of His holiness.

And he will delight in the fear of the Lord (Isaiah 11:3).

2. **P**ray for the wisdom and insight needed for the days ahead, grounded in the fear of the Lord.

He will be the sure foundation for your times, a rich store of salvation and wisdom and knowledge; the fear of the Lord is the key to this treasure (Isaiah 33:6).

3. **T**hank God for fighting on our behalf and displacing man's terror with a holy reverence for Him.

Do not call conspiracy everything this people calls a conspiracy; do not fear what they fear, and do not dread it. The Lord Almighty is the one you are to regard as holy, he is the one you are to fear, he is the one you are to dread (Isaiah 8:12-13).

DAY 3:

Purify Our Vision

> As we look not to the things that are seen but to the things that are unseen. For the things that are seen are transient, but the things that are unseen are eternal (2 Corinthians 4:18).

1. Pray for spiritual discernment to distinguish between good and evil, true and counterfeit.

They are from the world and therefore speak from the viewpoint of the world, and the world listens to them. We are from God, and whoever knows God listens to us; but whoever is not from God does not listen to us. This is how we recognize the Spirit of truth and the spirit of falsehood (1 John 4:5-6).

2. **P**ray that believers would discern according to the heart and spirit of a matter and not according to the flesh.

But the Lord said to Samuel, "Do not look at his appearance or at the height of his stature, because I have rejected him; for God sees not as man sees, for man looks at the outward appearance, but the Lord looks at the heart" (1 Samuel 16:7 NASB).

3. **P**ray that our judgment would be pure by the Spirit of the Lord.

He will not judge by what he sees with his eyes or decide by what he hears with his ears; but with righteousness he will judge the needy, with justice he will give decisions for the poor of the earth (Isaiah 11:3-4).

DAY 4:

Declare a Righteous Standard

> *Righteousness exalts a nation, but sin condemns any people* (Proverbs 14:34).

1. Pray that the Church would be free from cultural mind-molding and set apart unto the Lord.

Do not conform to the pattern of this world, but be transformed by the renewing of your mind. Then you will be able to test and approve what God's will is— his good, pleasing and perfect will (Romans 12:2).

2. **P**ray that believers would model a standard of holiness and righteousness for others to follow.

In the last days the mountain of the Lord's temple will be established as the highest of the mountains; it will be exalted above the hills, and peoples will stream to it (Micah 4:1).

3. **P**ray for the establishment of right and just rule in every sphere of the culture.

Righteousness and justice are the foundation of your throne; love and faithfulness go before you (Psalm 89:14).

DAY 5:

Establish Godly Rulers

> *I will restore your leaders as in days of old, your rulers as at the beginning. Afterward, you will be called the City of Righteousness, the Faithful City* (Isaiah 1:26).

1. Pray for God to raise up leaders with a passion for truth and empowered by the zeal of the Lord.

Moreover, look for able men from all the people, men who fear God, who are trustworthy and hate a bribe (Exodus 18:21 ESV).

2. **P**ray for leaders to be faithful to the truth and honor God's Word.

Those who walk righteously and speak what is right, who reject gain from extortion and keep their hands from accepting bribes, who stop their ears against plots of murder and shut their eyes against contemplating evil—they are the ones who will dwell on the heights, whose refuge will be the mountain fortress. Their bread will be supplied, and water will not fail them (Isaiah 33:15-16).

3. **A**sk that God remove those leaders whose life and witness do not honor Him or His Word.

The integrity of the upright guides them, but the unfaithful are destroyed by their duplicity (Proverbs 11:3).

DAY 6:

Become One in Mind and Spirit

> *Holy Father, protect them by the*
> *power of your name, the name you*
> *gave me, so that they may be one*
> *as we are one* (John 17:11).

1. **P**ray that the Church would hear the word of the Lord together and move as one.

I appeal to you, brothers and sisters, in the name of our Lord Jesus Christ, that all of you agree with one another in what you say and that there be no divisions among you, but that you be perfectly united in mind and thought (1 Corinthians 1:10).

2. **P**ray that each part of the Body would do their part, recognizing mutual need for one another.

But in fact God has placed the parts in the body, every one of them, just as he wanted them to be. If they were all one part, where would the body be? As it is, there are many parts, but one body (1 Corinthians 12:18-20).

3. **P**ray that the Church would rise up with one voice to drown out the counterfeit calls.

May the God who gives endurance and encouragement give you the same attitude of mind toward each other that Christ Jesus had, so that with one mind and one voice you may glorify the God and Father of our Lord Jesus Christ (Romans 15:5-6).

DAY 7:

Stand Against Evil

> *In him was life, and that life was the light of all mankind. The light shines in the darkness, and the darkness has not overcome it* (John 1:4-5).

1. Repent for any door that has been opened to the enemy due to pride, rebellion, or independence.

But you have planted wickedness, you have reaped evil, you have eaten the fruit of deception. Because you have depended on your own strength and on your many warriors (Hosea 10:13).

2. **P**ray for boldness to confront the darkness and renounce sinful practices and intents.

Who will rise up for me against the wicked? Who will take a stand for me against evildoers? (Psalms 94:16)

3. **P**ray that wicked practices would be exposed, bringing salvation and the fear of the Lord in power.

A number who had practiced sorcery brought their scrolls together and burned them publicly. …In this way the word of the Lord spread widely and grew in power (Acts 19:19-20).

DAY 8:

Call the Watchmen

> Lift up a banner against the walls
> of Babylon! Reinforce the guard,
> station the watchmen, prepare an
> ambush! The Lord will carry out his
> purpose, his decree against the people
> of Babylon (Jeremiah 51:12).

1. **B**less the watchmen and intercessors with increased wisdom, insight, and strategy.

Son of man, I have made you a watchman for the people of Israel; so hear the word I speak and give them warning from me (Ezekiel 3:17).

2. **P**ray for all who report the news, both secular and sacred, to speak that which is true and right.

Discretion will protect you, and understanding will guard you. Wisdom will save you from the ways of wicked men, from men whose words are perverse (Proverbs 2:11-12).

3. **P**ray for greater boldness in those called to stand watch in the nation, that they may speak God's Word clearly.

Go on up to a high mountain, O Zion, herald of good news; lift up your voice with strength, O Jerusalem, herald of good news; lift it up, fear not; say to the cities of Judah, "Behold your God!" (Isaiah 40:9 ESV)

DAY 9:

Ask for a Greater Outpouring of His Spirit

Blessed are those who have learned to acclaim you, who walk in the light of your presence, Lord. They rejoice in your name all day long; they celebrate your righteousness. For you are their glory and strength, and by your favor you exalt our horn (Psalms 89:15-17).

1. Pray for greater empowering of the Spirit to come to the Church.

And the Spirit of the Lord shall rest upon him, the Spirit of wisdom and understanding, the Spirit of counsel and might, the Spirit of knowledge and the fear of the Lord (Isaiah 11:2 ESV).

* *

2. **P**ray that the Church would display God's glory so that all will know He is God.

Then Moses said to him, "If your Presence does not go with us, do not send us up from here. How will anyone know that you are pleased with me and with your people unless you go with us? What else will distinguish me and your people from all the other people on the face of the earth?" (Exodus 33:15-16)

3. **P**ray for the fire of the Lord to fall on our land to bring transforming and healing power.

"And I myself will be a wall of fire around it," declares the Lord, "and I will be its glory within" (Zechariah 2:5).

DAY 10:

Bless All in Authority

> *Let everyone be subject to the governing
> authorities, for there is no authority
> except that which God has established.
> The authorities that exist have been
> established by God* (Romans 13:1).

1. **P**ray that our leaders would embrace godly
   wisdom and sound advice.

*For lack of guidance a nation falls, but victory is won
through many advisers* (Proverbs 11:14).

2. **P**ray for citizens to elect leaders who fear God, walk in integrity, and hate bribes.

But select capable men from all the people—men who fear God, trustworthy men who hate dishonest gain—and appoint them as officials over thousands, hundreds, fifties and tens (Exodus 18:21).

3. **B**less our elected leaders to do what is honorable before God and good for the people.

Therefore, you kings, be wise; be warned, you rulers of the earth. Serve the Lord with fear and celebrate his rule with trembling. Kiss his son, or he will be angry and your way will lead to your destruction, for his wrath can flare up in a moment. Blessed are all who take refuge in him (Psalms 2:10-12).

* *

DAY 11:

Bless the Increase of His Government

> *Your throne, O God, will last for ever and ever; a scepter of justice will be the scepter of your kingdom* (Psalms 45:6).

1. Rejoice in the supremacy of the Kingdom of God.

The Lord has established his throne in heaven, and his kingdom rules over all (Psalms 103:19).

2. **P**raise Him for His sovereignty over every nation of the earth, to His Father's glory.

He makes nations great, and destroys them; he enlarges nations, and disperses them (Job 12:23).

3. **T**hank Him for making our nation His inheritance.

Blessed is the nation whose God is the Lord, the people he chose for his inheritance (Psalms 33:12).

DAY 12:

Exalt His Name
Above Every Other Name

> *For God is the King of all the earth;*
> *sing to him a psalm of praise. God*
> *reigns over the nations; God is seated*
> *on his holy throne* (Psalms 47:7-8).

1. Declare that He, alone, is King.

   For kingship belongs to the Lord, and he rules over the nations (Psalms 22:28 ESV).

* *

2. **R**ejoice in His righteous judgment over every nation.

Who rules by his might forever, whose eyes keep watch on the nations—let not the rebellious exalt themselves (Psalms 66:7 ESV).

3. **D**eclare that every knee will bow and every tongue confess that He, alone, is God.

By myself I have sworn; from my mouth has gone out in righteousness a word that shall not return: "To me every knee shall bow, every tongue shall swear allegiance" (Isaiah 45:23 ESV).

TAKING THESE PRAYERS TO THE NEXT LEVEL

As you continue to pray through these twelve principles of righteous intercession, remember the power of corporate agreement. Though your personal prayer altar is necessary in starting the process, it's only when we pray about these things with other believers that our corporate authority will shift things in the spirit. When we are told in James 5:16 that the "...prayers of a righteous person are powerful and effective," it's within the context of healthy relationships and focused prayer with others. The power of our agreement is magnified when everyone has prepared their hearts ahead of time, gotten into alignment with their brothers and sisters, and cleared the path for corporate righteous intercession.

Consider these next steps in praying with others:

1. Share these twelve principles of righteous intercession with others in your church or community.

2. Join with a small group to focus on these prayer points. Determine to take each point to heart and invite the Holy Spirit to reveal more insight as you pray together on behalf of your community and the nation.

3. Consider a 12-day fast to coincide with these twelve points. The number twelve in Scripture often represents government and divine rule (see Rev. 21:12-14). Focus these prayers within your own fellowship in order to see God move on your behalf in your own church and community.

4. Consider going through these twelve prayer points with other churches in your community as a community-wide prayer initiative.

5. Ask the Lord for specific and targeted prayers that will bring tangible and measurable results. Expect the Lord to give practical application of these principles in your personal life, corporate life, and as a nation.

6. Incorporate additional prayer points from the remainder of this book to further your unity and vision.

Righteousness and justice are the foundation of your throne; love and faithfulness go before you. Blessed are those who have learned to acclaim you, who walk in the light of your presence, Lord. They rejoice in your name all day long; they celebrate your righteousness. For you are their glory and strength, and by your favor you exalt our horn (Psalms 89:14-17).

FIVE KEY
Prayer Strategies for
LASTING CHANGE

ONE of the challenges of intercession is maintaining the larger vision and purpose of our prayers. As we continue to pray for this nation in the midst of increased lawlessness, anarchy, and rebellion, it is easy to become discouraged and wonder if our prayers are working. However, God is working behind the scenes to do much more than simply address the troubling issues of the day. In His redemptive purposes, He uses the trials and setbacks, and even the enemy's attacks, to sanctify us, make us holy, and become more like

Himself (see Eph. 5:27). *Ultimately, He is not after our circumstances as much as He is after us. Until **we** are changed, the culture around us won't change.* The kind of transformation He desires always starts with His people.

And we all, who with unveiled faces contemplate the Lord's glory, are being transformed into His image with ever-increasing glory, which comes from the Lord, who is the Spirit (2 Corinthians 3:18).

Here are some considerations in our ongoing intercession as we seek to become a transformed people.

1. FOCUS OUR PRAYERS ON <u>DECLARING HIS PURPOSES</u> RATHER THAN ON <u>FIXING THE PROBLEMS</u>.

It's easy to get fixated on the issues at hand and forget His ultimate purpose in transformation. Until we can displace the godlessness with true righteousness through Christ, cycles of sin will continue. This requires a change of values and beliefs as we align our hearts and our prayers with His eternal Word.

+ Pray beyond the problem and declare His promise!

+ Pray God's heart and will over the situations at hand, and don't get distracted by the seeming discrepancies.

2. FOCUS OUR PRAYERS ON <u>GOD'S INCREASING KINGDOM</u> INSTEAD OF THE <u>WORLD'S CRUMBLING SYSTEMS</u>.

Apart from Christ, this world will continue to fall apart. We shouldn't be surprised at the failure of man's attempts to secure peace and freedom. God will continue to shake everything that can be shaken in order for the reality of His Kingdom to be clearly demonstrated through His people (see Heb. 12:27-28).

+ Instead of praying "against" things, pray for the purposes of God to prevail!

+ Spend time in worship and praise so that the King of glory may come in (see Ps. 24:9).

3. ADDRESS THE <u>SIN ISSUES</u> (DYING CARCASSES ON THE LAND) INSTEAD OF <u>FIGHTING THE DEVIL</u> (SHOOTING THE CIRCLING VULTURES).

The only reason our spiritual adversary has any foothold, both personally and corporately, is because of sin and unbelief. These attract the enemy just as rotting flesh on the ground attracts vultures. Rebuking the enemy (shooting the vultures) won't do any good if we don't deal with the sin (removing the flesh). Living a holy and righteous life is one of the best means of attracting heaven and repelling hell (see 2 Cor. 2:15; Eph. 5:2).

+ Pray for obedient hearts that quickly respond to His Word.

+ Pray that we would not only "turn from our wicked ways" but demonstrate holy lives that attract Heaven.

4. SHIFT FROM A <u>WARFARE MENTALITY</u> TO A <u>PRESENCE REALITY</u>.

Spiritual warfare may be necessary for a season but it was never intended to be a lifestyle. We were created to *live from* and *in* God's presence (see Acts 17:28; Isa. 63:9; Ps. 27:4-6). We need to remember the supernatural power of God's tangible presence (see Isa. 63:9). Throughout biblical history, the greatest victories came because of God's presence, not because of man's skills at warfare (the battle of Jericho in Joshua 6; Jehoshaphat's army in 2 Chronicles 20; the cloud of His presence at the Red Sea). There is no glory in battle. Our glory should be in the One who has already defeated the devil.

+ Spend time in celebrating the victory of our King and avoid fighting an enemy who has already lost.

5. KNOW THAT OUR SPIRITUAL AUTHORITY IN PRAYER COMES MORE FROM <u>WHO WE ARE</u> THAN FROM <u>WHAT WE PRAY</u>.

It is not the specific words of our prayers that change things but the condition of our hearts and the obedience of our walk. A transformed life is one that *loves* to do what we *ought* to do because we live, speak, and pray from a relationship that has radically changed us from the inside out. "*If you remain in me and my words remain in you, ask whatever you wish, and it will be done for you*" (John 15:7).

+ Ask the Lord for an undivided heart and purity of faith in which to pray and intercede.

+ Pray to become a living demonstration of the power and authority of the Kingdom right where you are.

In our desire to see things change in our nation, let us remember that *we* are the ones who must change first. The same power that raised Christ from the dead lives inside us and has power to bring new life to every nation and every tribe. As we are transformed, everything around us will begin to reflect the power of His Kingdom. Let our prayers reflect this goal.

THE CRY
for a Greater Outpouring of
THE HOLY SPIRIT
& Six Targeted Areas for Repentance

EVEN as we pray for national deliverance from the dark forces aligned against us, we must also consider the cost of maintaining our victory. Many are praying for a great outpouring of the Holy Spirit to permeate our land so that a fear of the Lord will awaken hearts and bring the lost to salvation. But we must also consider the cost of such a breakthrough. We must prepare our hearts and our lives for the needed changes and shifts that will be required to steward such an outpouring of His presence.

Salvation comes freely and God's grace is unmerited. However, preparing a place for a holy God to come and put things in order is something else. The visitations of past decades have been powerful preludes of what is to come, but the Church needs to consider the price tag to the pervasive and transforming spiritual revival that we desperately need.

Heaven is my throne, and the earth is my footstool. Where is the house you will build for me? Where will my resting place be? (Isaiah 66:1)

God is looking for a place to land, a place to build His habitation. If we truly want His righteousness to rule the land, we must prepare a place for His presence to dwell. If we are looking for God's presence and power to come to our cities and nation in order to redeem, restore, and transform—it's going to cost us. It will cost us personally and corporately. It will require giving up old mindsets in order to embrace the new wineskins He is preparing so that we can hold what He wants to pour out.

SIX TARGETED AREAS FOR REPENTANCE

The following issues have become roadblocks in our corporate pursuit of a great spiritual awakening. Pray through each of these and repent for any agreement with these attitudes, either personally or corporately.

1. Our Offenses

Unity in the Church is not just about denominational networking. It's about extending forgiveness to those who have hurt us—especially fellow believers. There are many who have left the Church out of offense. It's time to forgive and get plugged in again. The Lord has been calling back His "runaway brides." Those who have been hurt or overlooked in times past are being drawn back to the family of God to get re-attached, for the Body can't function without all the parts. Facing past issues will not always be easy. This will require humbling ourselves and embracing one another's faults and weaknesses in the journey.

> This outpouring will cost us our pride and the need to be right.

Jeremiah 9:23-24;
Matthew 5:23-25; James 4:6

2. Our Schedules

We have to stay together and walk together no matter what. We must learn to walk in commitment and not just when it's convenient. This applies at all levels—commitment to our spouse, commitment to our families, and, yes, commitment to the Body of Christ. This means that we determine to contribute our God-given role whenever it's needed—not just when it's convenient. We must choose to be faithful and consistent members of the Body of Christ, making it a priority rather than just another option.

> This outpouring will cost us our overloaded schedules.

Psalm 133; Romans 12:9-21;
1 Corinthians 12:12-26

3. Our Unhealthy Ties

Ungodly soul ties and generational curses can slowly drain us of the life of God until we revoke the legal ground of the enemy and receive God's intended blessings. Vows or oaths we have made to any group or individual that are not true to the Word of God will rob us of our spiritual inheritance and choke off our blessings and intimacy with Jesus. Our pursuit of holiness is not a religious ritual but a requirement to come before the presence of a Holy God.

> This outpouring will, more than likely, cost us some unhealthy relationships.

Deuteronomy 14:2; 2 Corinthians 6:14-18

4. Our Reputations

This is a team effort, which will require all the gifts and all hands on deck. Our culture desperately needs healthy spiritual fathers and mothers with a heart to raise up others to take their place. Servant leadership was God's idea, and it's what Jesus exemplified as He raised up spiritual sons and daughters to go further than He did. His greatest authority (and joy) came when He laid down His life and gave it away for others. God is looking for healthy leaders who care more about His house than their personal status. God will get all the glory when the world sees such leaders who serve rather than seek to be served.

> This outpouring will cost leaders any self-promoting reputation.

1 Corinthians 4:15; Philippians 2:1-11;
1 John 2:12-14

5. Our Lack of Patience

Sustained prayer and intercession require perseverance over the long haul. When we don't see immediate results, we get frustrated and either stop praying or try another prayer. Many times, God is simply inviting us to dig deeper in order to get to the roots of our issues. To Him, the process is just as important as the destination. The character, maturity, and spiritual insight that is gained through persistent prayer, study, and reflection brings us closer to His heart and ways. Jesus was always the hardest on His disciples as He challenged them in their thinking and perspectives. He wasn't as concerned with giving them the answers as He was with getting to their hearts.

> This outpouring will cost us
> our need for quick fixes.

Romans 5:1-5; 8:26-30; Hebrews 6:11-12

6. Our Time

The Lord is looking for a place like home. For Heaven to come to earth, we must prepare that place for Him to come. This is not just allegory but actual. Cities, congregations, and ministries that have already experienced a measure of His manifest presence testify to the power of preparing such a place. This should be normal for the Church—the starting place for lasting transformation! Are we willing to host Heaven and prepare a place for Him to not only visit, but stay? Are we willing to prepare the sanctuary and our schedules to make room for Him to come as we wait in His presence? Are we willing to become like the five virgins who took the time to fill their lamps with oil, readying themselves for the Bridegroom?

> ## This outpouring will cost us our time.

Exodus 33:14-16; 1 Samuel 3;
Isaiah 57:14-15; 66:1

Pray through each of these concerns personally but, more importantly, as a community of believers. Consider how to adjust your mindsets and expectations in order to align with God's heart and purposes as the Church. Go beyond repentance to seeking new beliefs and practices to displace that which is unhealthy, ungodly, and lacking in spiritual power. Determine to become new wineskins, able to hold that which God wants to release at all levels of our society.

God *is* coming with another awakening of His love and power, but this time it will be something much bigger than just revival. It will be total transformation. He's coming to bring life-changing and lasting reformation to the earth and that means we need to get our houses ready to sustain His presence. He can't entrust His presence to orphans or slaves. He is looking for sons and daughters who know who they are and are ready to carry His heart for the sake of the Kingdom.

We are not just preparing to bring in the lost, save a city, or deliver a nation. We are preparing to live with a Holy God whose presence is overwhelming, life-changing, and supernatural. It will be worth the cost.

A Prayer
for President Trump

On June 2, 2019, Franklin Graham issued a call to the Church to set aside a day to pray for our President. This prayer was used by thousands in lifting up President Trump. Continue to use this, both individually and corporately, as a prayer of blessing over the highest office in the land.

Heavenly Father,

We come as the body of Christ in this nation to lift up our President, Donald J. Trump. As many voices rise up against this one You have set into office, we lift up our voices, with one heart and mind, to stand in agreement with heaven's purposes concerning our nation (Ps. 133). **We stand by this President who has declared this nation to be under God's rule and authority** and we seek righteousness and justice for our nation (Ps. 89:14).

We welcome and embrace the fear of the Lord as the standard for all righteous rule and repent for the ways in which we have bowed to the fear of man. Cleanse our hearts and renew our minds that we may walk in the light of Your truth (Ps. 43:3). **We ask that President Trump would delight in the fear of the Lord** in order to walk in the power of Your might and the wisdom of Your ways (Mic. 3:8). May righteousness and faithfulness be his portion so that he may render righteous judgments according to Your Word (Isa. 11:3-5).

We ask that President Trump would show no fear toward the evil that assails him (Isa. 8:12) but rather overcome it with a zeal and passion for Your *laws which bring life and liberty to all (Prov. 10:29-32).* **May he love Your Word** *and seek your wisdom diligently (Prov. 8:17), remaining open and teachable to godly counsel and heaven's wisdom (Prov. 1:7). We thank You that his heart is in Your hands and that You will direct it according to Your will and purpose.* **Grant him increased grace and blessing** *as he heeds your voice and obeys Your word (Prov. 21:1).*

We declare over President Trump that he will have true judgments by the Spirit *and not according to man (Isa. 11:3-4). We declare that he will possess heaven's knowledge with shrewdness of mind in making right decisions for the good of the people (Prov. 8:12). Fill his mouth with good things (Prov. 16:9-13) that he may speak what is true and right (Prov. 8:6). We pray that he will* **use his God-given authority to execute justice** *and establish righteousness in this land for the sake of Your glory and Kingdom. (Gen. 49:10; Ps. 60:7).* **We declare that he will rule in the midst of his enemies, not backing down or wavering due to threats or**

intimidation (Ps. 110:1-2; Eph. 6:13). May his ears become deaf to the assaults from his enemies and may those who seek his life answer to You for their wicked ways. May he know that it is Your hand and Your sovereign purpose that is keeping him and sustaining him in his divine commission (Ps. 38:12-15).

Keep President Trump, and those who serve him, safe *from the enemy's snares and free from the accuser's traps (Ps. 141:9-10). By Your great hand, Lord, deal with those who oppose righteousness and justice so that all men will know it is You alone who is sovereign and true (Ps. 64:6-9).* **May the fire of Your presence burn up all Your enemies** *and consume all those who stand against You concerning our destiny and inheritance as one nation under God (Ps. 97:1-6).*

Thank You, Father, for hearing our prayers *and empowering us as Kingdom ambassadors on the earth.* **From the highest office in the land to the least known among men, may we all seek to know You more intimately, serve You more passionately, and**

praise You more fully so that all men will be saved.
Through the name of Your Son, Jesus Christ, we pray.
Amen.

A PROPHETIC
Charge to the
CHURCH:

**MOVING FROM SWORD TO SCEPTER: RULING
THROUGH PRAYER AS THE EKKLESIA OF GOD**

Excerpt from the upcoming book
Moving from Sword to Scepter

IN a recent time of prayer concerning the battles at hand in this nation and how to effectively intercede, I heard in my spirit, "It is time to move from the *sword* to the *scepter*." As I continued to pray into this, I sensed the Lord calling intercessors to consider another strategy in dealing with the demonic forces coming against believers in this hour. I believe the prayer movement is transitioning from the position of being *warriors* to a position of being *rulers*.

A familiar weapon of our warfare has been the sword of the Lord, the Word of God (see Heb. 4:12). However, the Word of the Lord can be wielded not only with a sword in battle but with a scepter from the throne. A scepter symbolizes a king's judicial authority and is usually given as an inheritance, handed from father to son. **We are shifting into a time of Kingdom rule where the primary tool in establishing His Kingdom will be the scepter.**

Your throne, O God, will last for ever and ever; a scepter of justice will be the scepter of your kingdom (Psalm 45:6).

As we recognize who we are as sons and daughters of the King and lay claim to the promised land that is ours on the earth (see Ps. 115:16), we can take our place seated with Him (see Eph. 2:6). Even as enemy forces are being displaced and dethroned across the globe, the focus must shift from the battlefield into the throne room where kingly rule takes place.

A warrior tends to focus on the battle and the strength needed to defeat an enemy. In a spiritual confrontation, much time and energy can be expended in assuming the posture of a warrior instead of a ruler. Even in current prophetic intercession, there is the temptation to believe the volume of our prayers, the passion of our cries, or the force of our delivery will somehow defeat the devil. **If we believe our victory is secured because of our own merits as a warrior, our identity and call is misplaced.** Our spiritual adversary is determined to wear out many intercessors through needless battles unless we change our strategy.

We can begin to defeat the enemy through exe-cuting righteous judgments from the throne room instead of fighting with him on the battlefield.

It is a shift in the posture of our hearts. It is a shift in the attitude of our prayers. It is a shift in our identities as we secure our inheritance, not because we have *fought* for it or *earned* it, but because He has *given it to us* (see Col. 1:12). We take our posi-tion, not with a sword in hand ready to do battle but with a scepter in hand ready to render decisions.

When a storm, driven by a demonic principal-ity, tore over the lake where Jesus and the disciples were, Jesus stood in the boat and simply spoke three words: "Peace! Be still!" There was no battle. There was no struggle. Only a word. This is the kind of authority that is ours if we but believe.

And he awoke and rebuked the wind and said to the sea, "Peace! Be still!" And the wind ceased, and there was a great calm. He said to them, "Why are you so afraid? Have you still no faith?" (Mark 4:39-40)

When the spiritual opposition rages all around us, we must remember who and *whose* we are. The victory over our enemies has been settled and we are seated with Christ in heavenly places. As Christ was given the scepter with which to rule over His enemies, so we can partner with His purposes in prayer.

The Lord says to my lord: "Sit at my right hand until I make your enemies a footstool for your feet." The Lord will extend your mighty scepter from Zion, saying, "Rule in the midst of your enemies!" (Psalm 110:1-2)

Within our nation, we are currently seeing a demonstration of the prophetic mandate to *"uproot and tear down, to destroy and overthrow"* in order to *"build and to plant"* (see Jer. 1:10). Even as the highest office in the land is actively doing this in clearing out corruption and wickedness, so are many prophetic intercessors responding to this call to uproot demonic systems and strongholds. Yet the Lord is calling us to do this work from the throne as the primary means of executing justice. We are to remember the authority granted to us by the King of kings in rendering righteous decisions and disarming the enemy. This authority is ours because of our position in Christ, not because of our strength or abilities as prophetic warriors.

But with righteousness he will judge the needy, with justice he will give decisions for the poor of the earth. He will strike the earth with the rod of his mouth; with the breath of his lips he will slay the wicked (Isaiah 11:3-4).

Spiritual warfare is not as much about the strength or performance of the warrior as it is about the supremacy and authority of the King. Kings have nothing to prove. Rulers do not strive to be known. Jesus knew who He was when He spoke to the storm. He was not looking to build a reputation or a ministry through His performance as a prophet. He simply stood up and agreed with His Father.

THE CHALLENGE WE FACE

Though we don't like to admit it, most of us are stirred to increased prayer and action when there's a crisis. The globalist agenda and demonic influence at work in our nation is now manifesting in city squares and community halls, and the grass roots movement is rising up. Not only are Christians crying out for a change, but anyone who sees past the smoke screen of political correctness is going to the streets demanding change.

As much as we have rejoiced in the breakthrough of 2016 and the Cyrus anointing at work in the White House, the critical question remains: Can we occupy the land and steward the victory long term, or are we still too weak, too divided, and too immature to take our place? How many national crises and divisive elections will it take to turn this nation around for good?

WE NEED A LEGACY

What will our descendants say about our watch? Have we prematurely celebrated entering our promised land of prophetic promises and Holy Spirit manifestations without addressing the squatting giants in the land? Do we have the courage to run into enemy territory to take down the demonic behemoths or will we stay on the edge of our inheritance secretly hoping for Heaven's cavalry to come rescue us from the battle?

We don't only need to turn our nation "back"; we need to disciple this nation toward maturity. We need to grow up. The cultural shifts needed and ungodly beliefs to be overturned are deep—and that's just in the Church! They will require not only persevering faith and targeted prayer, but practical application at every level of society—for

years to come. If we want to see long-term transformation, it will require a coming together of
generations, ethnicities, genders, and values. It will
require leaders with integrity and a vision for the
future. It will require a prophetic perspective of
the Kingdom now in order to keep the territory
we so desperately want to take.

For those with the courage to face the challenge,
it's time to put our prayers into action, become
strategic in our warfare, and take our place as
Kingdom leaders in this nation. Without appro-
priate action and demonstration of that which we
pray for, nothing will truly change. Until we have
a clear mission of the Ekklesia and a viable vision
for the future, we will continue to go around this
mountain of indecision and division and never
occupy until He comes.

Even as deep darkness continues to cover
the earth and wicked rulers challenge Kingdom
authority, believers must position themselves in
prayer in a new way. Rather than getting stuck on

the battlefield in endless skirmishes sent to distract us, we must learn how and when to lay down the sword and take up His scepter. The Church has learned how to "war in the spirit" but we must also learn how to rule in the midst of our enemies.

★ ★ ★

In her upcoming book, *Moving from the Sword to the Scepter*, Wanda Alger calls the Church to a prophetic perspective on the state of the Church and how to prepare for the days ahead. The following are some of the main issues and questions addressed in the book, which will include prayer guides and resources to equip and empower believers and communities to take, keep, and occupy their own territory for the Kingdom:

Ruling in the Midst of Our Enemies
(Shining Lights in the Midst of Deep Darkness)

Do we have the courage to rule in the middle of enemy territory? Are we truly prepared to face the coming evil with fearless confidence in the Lord? Our corporate vision for the future will determine if and how well we rule.

Are We Qualified to Rule?
(Influence and Authority Are Earned)

Is all spiritual authority equal? Do intercessors know their unique fields of authority, or have we mistakenly opened the door to the enemy through presumption and spiritual posturing? Governmental prayer requires specific protocols and believers must recognize the various levels of authority and corporate agreement necessary in order for our prayers to bring results.

The Rising Ecclesia and God's Government
(What Is Kingdom Government?)

Are we packing to leave or positioned to lead? Are pastors and church leaders modeling Kingdom government that shifts atmospheres and cities? Until we embrace the call to lead the way through our own example, starting in the Church, wicked rulers will continue to reign.

A Legacy to Fight For
(From Prophetic Potential to Gaining Our Inheritance)

How is the Church discipling this nation? Do we have a vision that goes beyond our current generation? Abraham fathered a nation because he discipled three generations in order to establish the foundation of Israel. Spiritual fathers and mothers are desperately needed in this hour to establish spiritual houses across the nation that will endure and stand the test of time.

The Word and the Spirit Coming Together
(Apostolic Authority and Prophetic Power)

Can charismatics and evangelicals find common ground for the sake of the Kingdom? Can mercy and truth co-exist as we seek conservative values in our laws and practices? Until we deal with corporate offenses that have weakened our unity as the body of Christ, we will have limited influence and ineffective prayers.

Watchmen to Their Posts
(Intercessors to the Airways!)

Do we only pray when there's a crisis? How do we engage more believers in the secret place in order to host the presence of the Lord? Where do we get our intel from for effective prayer? There are watchmen both secular and sacred who are responsible for sounding the alarm. We must raise the standard in our reporting and bring fresh accountability to those with prophetic eyes and ears.

Righteous Rule Must Be Modeled
(The Desperate Need for Leadership)

How is the Church raising up healthy leaders? Are five-fold equippers embraced and released within the Church to mature and mobilize the saints within all the spheres of our culture? Until we learn to trust our leaders and build healthy teams, we will be crippled in our influence and authority in the public square.

Moving from the Sword to the Scepter
(From Warriors to Rulers)

What's the difference between a warrior and a ruler? How do we keep, guard, and occupy our local ground, much less our national sovereignty? We must learn the practical application of these principles and make it a lifestyle, not just a method.

Warfare That Works
(Practices from the Early Church)

Has our understanding of spiritual warfare in the past generation brought the results we need? Have we gotten stuck in one method of combat and forgotten the battle plan? Our nation doesn't just need deliverance from principalities and spiritual rulers in high places, but a displacement by a united Ecclesia with corporate authority. We must engage in warfare that works—the early Church showed us how—and it's not what you think.

From Reformation to Transformation
(The Sudden Shift That's Coming)

What's the difference between revival and reformation? Are we praying for a quick fix or a complete makeover? The Lord has been giving clues to prophetic voices as to what is coming, and we must prepare for the supernatural realities about to occur.

The Mordecai Mandate (Securing Your City)

Is your city or community secured for the Kingdom? Is there a local coalition that is engaged in the public square and partnering with the Church for conservative Christian values? Before we can see lasting change at the national level, we must learn to occupy our own communities. Apostolic leadership in every mountain of culture is critical in leading the charge.

BUY THE NEW BOOK

Moving from Sword to Scepter,
from Destiny Image available in February 2020 wherever books are sold.

Additional
Resources

R EADY to mobilize and join others who are
praying for the nation? Go to ifapray.org for
these free tools and resources:

**Find out where others are praying near you on this
interactive prayer map:**

Join the 24/7 Interactive Prayer Wall for the Nation:

Look for daily updates on how to pray concerning news headlines, national and state issues, and the Church's response from a prophetic perspective:

 Headline Prayer: News Christians need to pray about *EVERY DAY*

 FRANKLIN GRAHAM CALLS FOR DAY OF PRAYER FOR PRES. TRUMP SUNDAY, JUNE 2

MAY 31, 2019

> Heavenly Father, let there be a loud cry of support for our President this Sunday...

Evangelist, Franklin Graham is calling Christians across the nation to join him and other leaders in a day of prayer for President Trump this Sunday, June 2. In his Facebook...

 LOUISIANA DEMOCRATIC GOVERNOR SIGNS HEARTBEAT BILL

MAY 31, 2019

> Thank you Lord, for this governor, who is standing firm for life, even against his...

As Louisiana joins the ranks of states passing heartbeat abortion bans, the case is highlighting a growing effort by Democrat leaders to reject all pro-lifers from their party. Louisiana's Democratic...

 WHY ARE SOME PRO-LIFE MINISTRIES AND LEADERS FIGHTING TO KEEP ABORTION?

MAY 31, 2019

> Lord, forgive us for our inability to grasp that simply restricting abortion still accepts it....

The fight challenging the legality of abortion has never been more intense. Every month new laws are brought to a vote across our land as state after state reveals their...

★★★

Join IFA's growing Facebook community for up-to-the-minute reporting, prayer strategies, and interaction with believers across the nation:

Receive weekly email alerts to inform and empower your prayers:

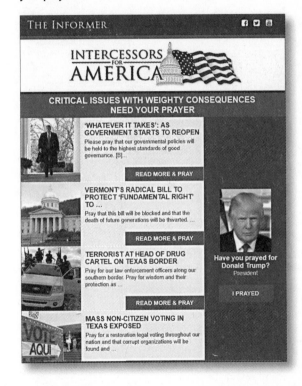

THE INFORMER

INTERCESSORS FOR AMERICA

CRITICAL ISSUES WITH WEIGHTY CONSEQUENCES NEED YOUR PRAYER

'WHATEVER IT TAKES': AS GOVERNMENT STARTS TO REOPEN

Please pray that our governmental policies will be held to the highest standards of good governance. [B]...

READ MORE & PRAY

VERMONT'S RADICAL BILL TO PROTECT 'FUNDAMENTAL RIGHT' TO ...

Pray that this bill will be blocked and that the death of future generations will be thwarted. ...

READ MORE & PRAY

TERRORIST AT HEAD OF DRUG CARTEL ON TEXAS BORDER

Pray for our law enforcement officers along our southern border. Pray for wisdom and their protection as ...

READ MORE & PRAY

Have you prayed for Donald Trump?
President

I PRAYED

MASS NON-CITIZEN VOTING IN TEXAS EXPOSED

Pray for a restoration legal voting throughout our nation and that corrupt organizations will be found and ...

Download free devotionals, prayer guides, and articles by going to ifapray.org and clicking on resources.

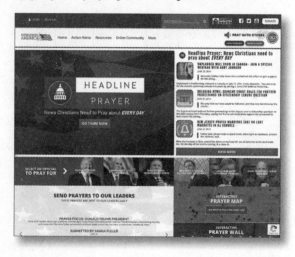

About
Wanda Alger

WANDA Alger is a recognized five-fold prophetic minister with DOVE USA and field correspondent with Intercessors for America. The author of three books, she also maintains her own blog (wandaalger.me) and has had her articles published with Charisma, The Christian Post, Spirit Fuel, and The Elijah List. Her husband pastors Crossroads Community Church in Winchester, Virginia, which they planted in 1998. They have three adult children.

Stay up-to-date by following my blog at wandaalger.me